Mel Bay Presents

Mandolin Christmas Songbook

Arranged By
Lee "Drew" Andrews

This book may be used along with *Mel Bay's Ukulele Christmas Songbook* (MB20886). All songs, except "Away in a Manger," are in the same key and can be played together. Most songs in *Mel Bay's Tenor Banjo Christmas Songbook* (MB21014) are also in the same keys and can be used together.

1 2 3 4 5 6 7 8 9 0

Visit us on the Web at www.melbay.com — E-mail us at email@melbay.com

Contents

Angels We Have Heard On High

Traditional

An - gels we have heard on high sweet - ly sing - ing o'er the plains.

And the moun - tains in re - ply ech - o - ing their joy - ous strains.

Glo - - - - - - - - - - - - ri - a in ex - cel - sis

De - o Glo - - - - - - - - - - - ri - a

in ex - cel - sis De - - - - o.

Auld Lang Syne

Traditional

Should auld ac - quaint - ance be for - got, and nev - er brought to

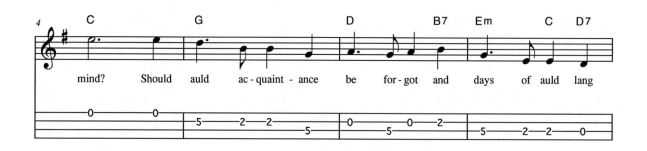

mind? Should auld ac - quaint - ance be for - got and days of auld lang

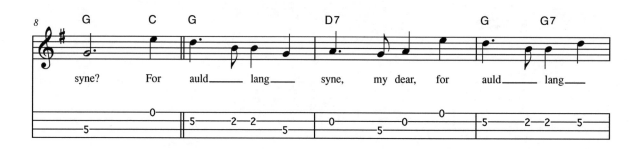

syne? For auld lang syne, my dear, for auld lang

syne we'll take a cup of kind - ness yet, for auld lang syne.

Away in a Manger

Traditional

A - way in a man - ger no crib for a

bed, the lit - tle Lord Je - sus laid down his sweet

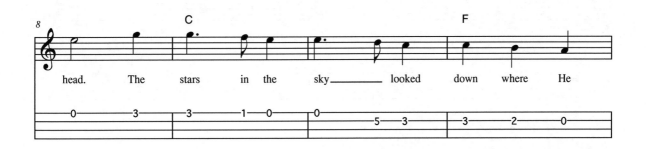

head. The stars in the sky___ looked down where He

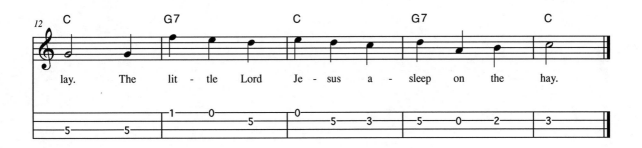

lay. The lit - tle Lord Je - sus a - sleep on the hay.

Bring a Torch, Jeannette, Isabella

Traditional

Deck the Halls

Traditional

Deck the halls with boughs of hol - ly Fa la la la la la la la la.

'Tis the sea - son to be jol - ly. Fa la la la la la la la la.

Don we now our gay ap - par - el. Fa la la la la la la la.

Troll the an - cient yule - tide car - ol. Fa la la la la la la la la.

The First Noel

Traditional

Go Tell it on the Mountain

Traditional

When I was a sin - ner, I prayed both night and day; I

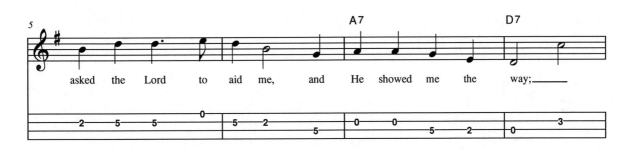

asked the Lord to aid me, and He showed me the way;_____

Go tell it on the moun - tain, o - ver the hills and ev - ery - where;

go tell it on the moun - tain, that Je - sus Christ___ is born.

God Rest Ye Merry Gentlemen

Traditional

God rest ye mer - ry, gen - tle - men; let noth - ing you dis - may. Re -

mem - ber, Christ our Sav - ior was born on Christ - mas Day to save us all from

Sa - tan's pow'r when we were gone a - stray. O___ ti - dings of com - fort and

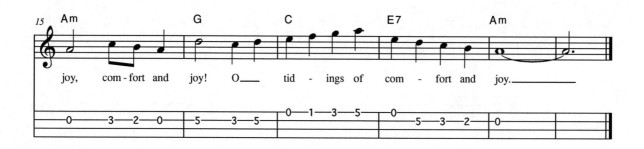

joy, com - fort and joy! O___ tid - ings of com - fort and joy.___

Good King Wenceslas

Traditional

Hark! The Herald Angels Sing

Mendelssohn/Wesley

The Holly and the Ivy

Traditional

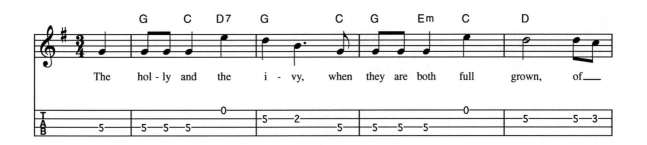

The hol - ly and the i - vy, when they are both full grown, of___

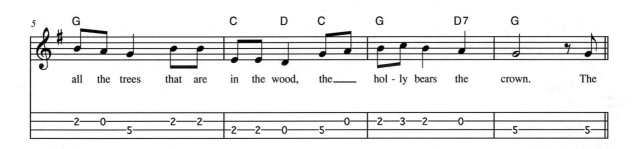

all the trees that are in the wood, the___ hol - ly bears the crown. The

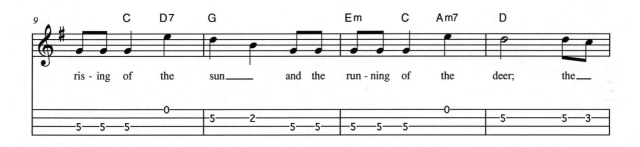

ris - ing of the sun___ and the run - ning of the deer; the___

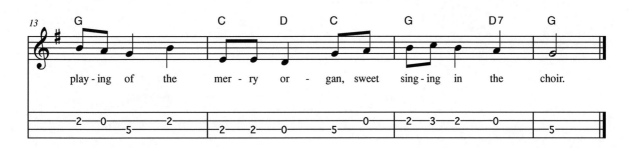

play - ing of the mer - ry or - gan, sweet sing - ing in the choir.

I Saw Three Ships

Traditional

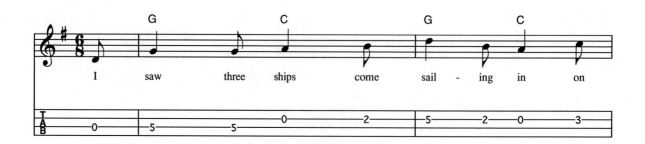

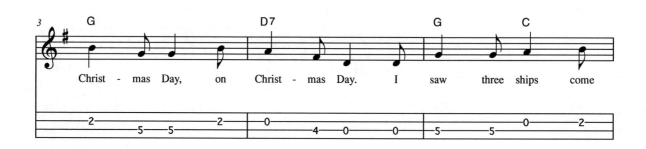

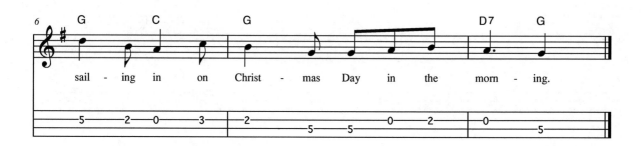

It Came Upon a Midnight Clear

Traditional

Jingle Bells

Traditional

Jolly Old Saint Nicholas

Traditional

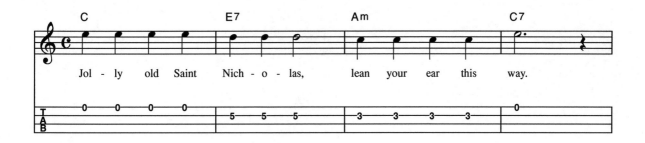

Jol - ly old Saint Nich - o - las, lean your ear this way.

Don't you tell a sin - gle soul what I'm going to say.

Christ - mas Eve is com - ing soon. Now, my dear old man,

whis - per what you'll bring to me; tell me if you can.

Joy to the World

Mason/Watts

O Christmas Tree

Traditional

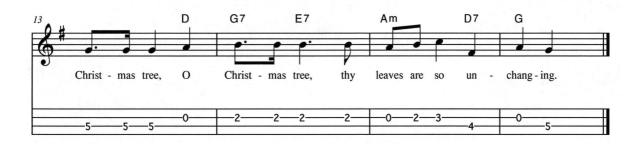

19

O Come, All Ye Faithful

J. Reading

O Come, O Come Emmanuel

Traditional

O Little Town of Bethlehem

Lewis H. Redner

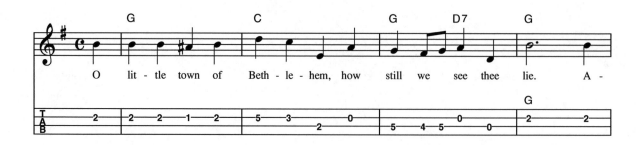

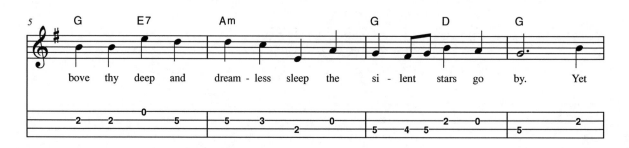

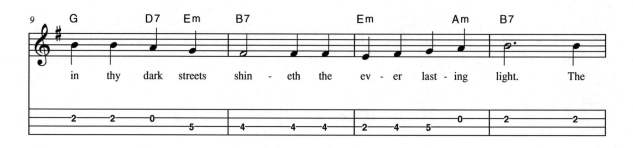

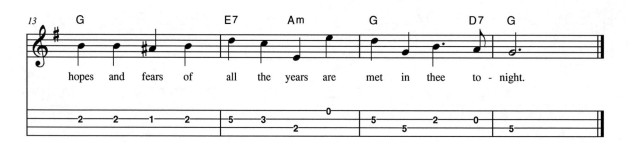

Silent Night

Traditional

Toyland

MacDonough/Herbert

Up On the Housetop

Benjamin Russell Hanby

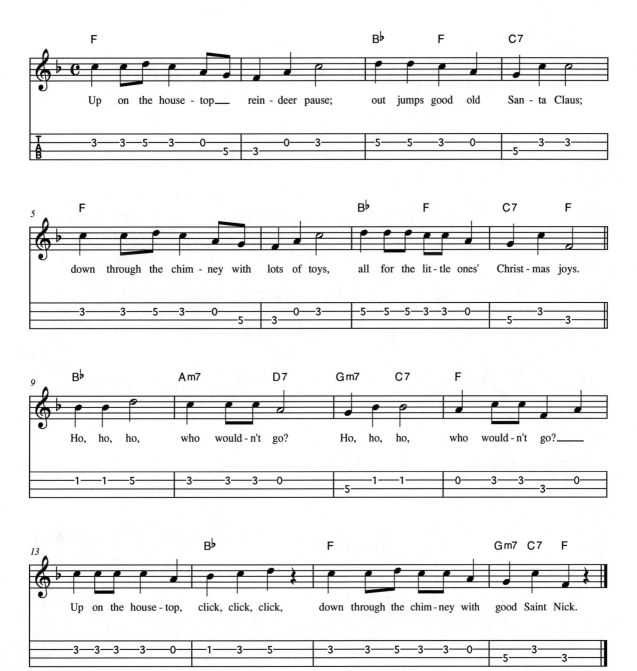

We Three Kings of Orient Are

John H. Hopkins

We Wish You a Merry Christmas

Traditional

What Child is This?

Traditional English

While Shepherds Watched Their Flocks by Night

Traditional

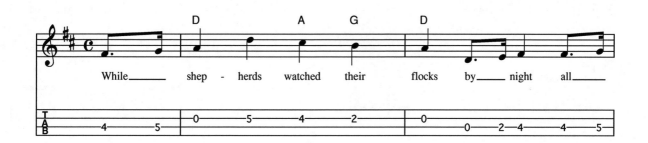

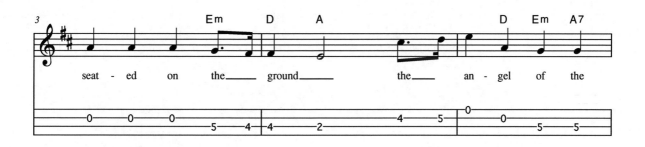

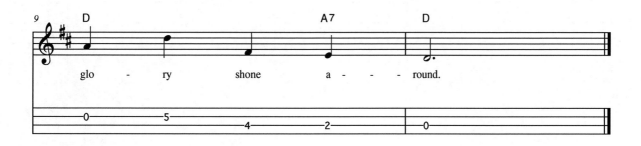

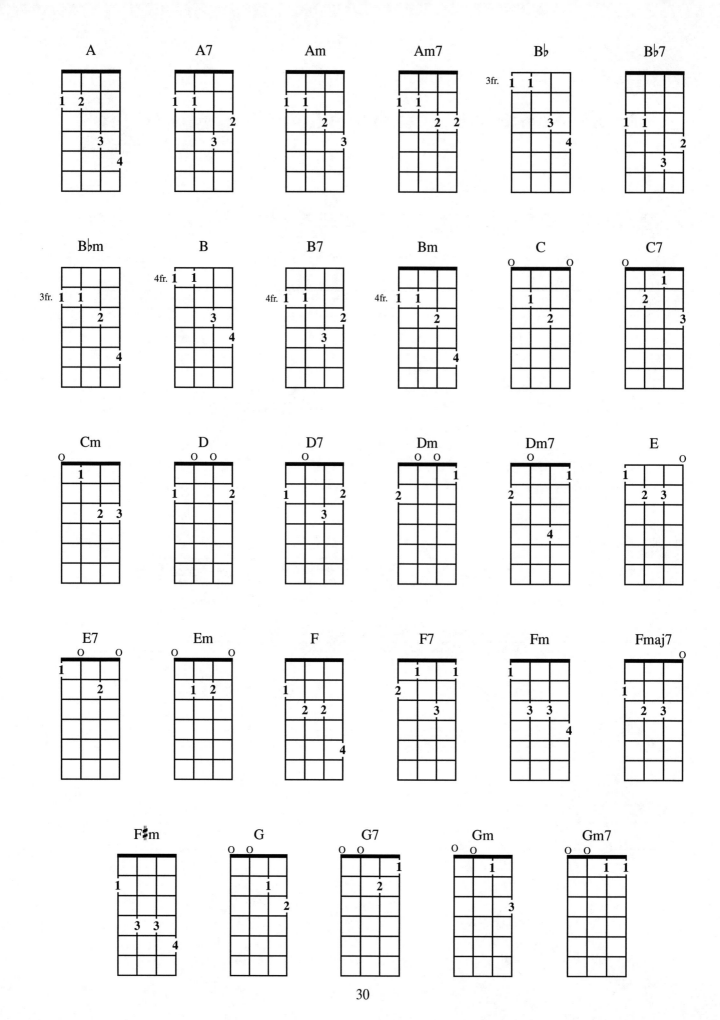

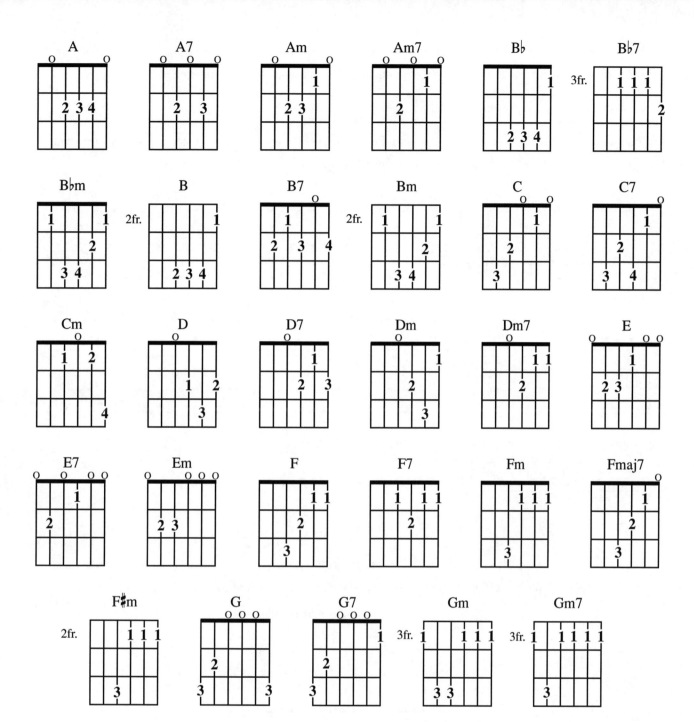

Written below are eight strum patterns. Each of the strum patterns takes one measure of 4/4 or 3/4 to complete and can be used with any tune. Once a pattern has been selected, play the same pattern in each measure of the piece.

◻ = Strum down.   V = Strum up.

Practice holding any chord and play each pattern. Be careful to use the correct strum direction and correct rhythm. Tap you foot on each beat and count the rhythms aloud. The patterns are written in order of difficulty.

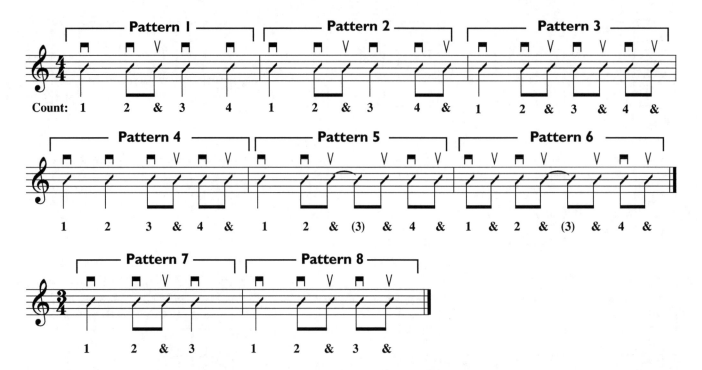

Notice pattern six contains a loop called a "tie". When two strum bars or two of the same notes are connected with a tie, play the first strum and allow it to ring through the time value of the second. Do not strum the second strum bar.

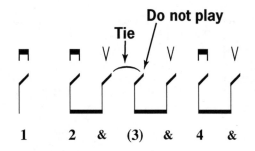

When two chords appear in a measure with more active strum patterns, simply repeat the process for two chords in a measure for down strums only. If a strum pattern has a tie between beats two and three, it is common to anticipate the second chord in the measure by playing it on the "and" of two.

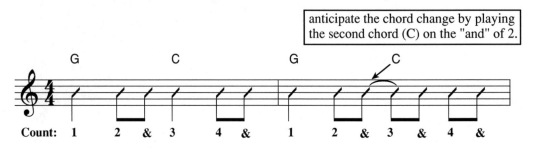